THE *CHRYSEMYS* MESS

This book is intended to be an overview of the about 15 species related to the Painted Turtle, *Chrysemys picta*, of North America (family Emydidae, the emydid turtles). This group includes the very familiar Red-eared Slider, *Trachemys scripta elegans*, the best-known pet turtle in the world, its relatives in the Caribbean and tropical America, and also a number of related species from North America usually called cooters and red-bellied turtles. I've also thrown in a chapter on the Chicken Turtle, *Deirochelys reticularia*, of the southern United States because the similarities to the Paint are obvious...and I happen to like this turtle a lot.

These turtles have been studied intensively for decades, and many are very well-known. *Trachemys scripta* even has an entire scientific monograph devoted to it and covering all aspects of its life in great detail, more detail than any hobbyist would ever want to read. There is a major mess, however, concerning the relationships of these turtles to each other, what I call "the *Chrysemys* mess."

CHRYSEMYS VERSUS THE WORLD

Anyone with half an eye can look at a Painted Turtle, the Slider Turtle, and a Cooter and make a pretty good guess that they are closely related. They share similar body forms (the upper shell or carapace varies from somewhat flattened to domed but always gives the same impression), similar color patterns (green to black skin with yellow stripes on the head, neck, legs, and tail), elongated male foreclaws in species from north of the Rio Grande that are used to stroke the face of the female during courtship, and generally similar natural histories. Their skeletons

PHOTO: W. P. MARA.

Like these Siamese twin Red-eared Sliders, *Trachemys scripta elegans*, taxonomists have been pulled in many directions while trying to determine the relationships of the cooters and sliders.

are virtually identical, the differences mostly concerned with the development of the jaws for chopping meat or plants and the number of bones in the toes. Some species have nearly smooth shells, while others have strongly developed wrinkles or rugosities.

These turtles have a long fossil history in North America, and there are indications that three groups (we'll disregard the Chicken Turtle

For many years all three groups were considered to belong to a single genus, *Chrysemys*, or at best two: *Chrysemys* and *Pseudemys*. Over the last decade or so, however, increasing evidence from molecular biology, study of parasites (yes, parasites evolve along with their hosts, so separate genera often have distinctive groups of parasites),

PHOTO: M. P. & C. PIEDNOIR.

The red ear or postorbital stripe of *Trachemys scripta elegans* has made it one of the most recognizable turtles. This feature is shared with many tropical sliders, however, so not every turtle with a red ear is a Red-ear.

for now since scientists are about equally split on whether it is related to the Paint or to *Emys*; I plunk down solidly for the Paint relationship) long have been distinct and evolving separately. These groups are the Painted Turtles, *Chrysemys*; the cooters and red-bellies, *Pseudemys*; and the sliders, *Trachemys*.

mathematical models of shell development, and new looks at the anatomy of these turtles have led many specialists to insist that the three groups represent three distinct genera. I have to admit that I personally have doubts about this because there is no way to adequately define *Pseudemys* and *Trachemys* except

A gorgeous albinistic Red-eared Slider, *Trachemys scripta elegans*. These colorful mutants are being bred in small numbers but remain expensive centerpieces of any aquatic turtle collection.

by just listing the characters of their species rather than real generic characters that could be seen in the skull or skeleton. However, I'm going with the flow in this book and not being a maverick—there are three genera of turtles discussed here.

THE GENERA

Painted Turtles (*Chrysemys*) are small (seldom over 6 inches, 15 cm), rather low-shelled turtles in which the back of the carapace is smooth and unnotched (the marginals are not indented at the edges) and the plastron is yellow with or without dark lines. The edges of the carapace are bright red (sometimes more yellowish). The upper jaw has a central notch flanked on each side by a cusp or pseudotooth.

Cooters (*Pseudemys*) are large, often greatly domed turtles that are brown to greenish brown in adults, often with a distinct yellowish C or vertical stripe on the second costal scute. The rear edge of the carapace is serrated (sometimes almost worn smooth in old adult females). The jaws are variously cusped, notched, and serrated, or not, and if looked at from the front the lower jaw is flat on the underside. There never is a large red spot behind the eye, and adult males of all species have long foreclaws.

Sliders (*Trachemys*) also may be large, highly domed turtles that are brown to greenish brown in adults, and they often have vertical yellow lines on the second costal scute. The rear edge of the carapace is serrated. The upper

jaw may be notched in the center or not, but there are not flanking cusps. Looked at from the front, the lower jaw appears distinctly rounded underneath. Many species and subspecies have a widened stripe or isolated spot behind the eye that is distinct from the other stripes on the head and often has a dull reddish brown to bright red center. Old males (and sometimes females) of most species and subspecies tend to become more or less dark brown (melanistic), obscuring the pattern of the head and shell. Males of forms north of the Rio Grande and in the Caribbean usually have long foreclaws, while those of forms from northern Mexico to Uruguay have short claws like females.

As you can see, it is impossible to accurately distinguish the genera on characters of the shell and head, as in most other turtles, and you must tell the genus by identifying the species.

GENERAL CARE

Most Paints and relatives have very similar natural histories that differ in details often related to adult size and the climate cycles of the areas in which they live. This makes their care in the aquarium or aquaterrarium similar as well. Care of the Red-eared Slider, *Trachemys scripta elegans*, has been covered in detail in Patterson's book, *Red-eared Slider Turtles* (T.F.H., RE-109), and that book is recommended if you want to keep any species talked about in this book.

First, the Salmonella Laws

Sliders and cooters are most attractive as juveniles, usually becoming darker and less distinctly patterned (especially on the shell) as they mature. Until 1975, baby Red-eared Sliders and four or five other species (including southern Painted established in many ponds and lakes in the northern United States, Europe, and Japan, as well as oases in Arabia and pools in South Africa. The sale of hatchlings was wasteful of animals, but no one seemed to care.

Following several cases of

A male Florida Red-bellied Turtle, *Pseudemys nelsoni*. The long claws are characteristic of adult males of most northern cooters and sliders and may even be visible in quite small young over 4 inches (10 cm) in shell length.

PHOTO: R. D. BARTLETT.

Turtles, some cooters, plus map turtles) were gathered by the thousands in turtle farms in Louisiana and adjacent areas and sold to the pet trade throughout the world. Because babies are very difficult to keep, almost all died within weeks or months, and those that adapted often grew large enough to discourage the keeper, who released them into local waters. Red-ears became salmonellosis in children in the early 1970's, the American Food and Drug Administration (FDA) caused laws to be enacted in 1975 that prohibited the shipment of small turtles across state borders in the United States and also restricted their sale in the United States. Salmonellosis is an intestinal disease caused by a multitude

Though American health laws prohibit the sale of turtles under 4 inches (10 cm) in carapace length, it is not illegal in most areas to collect your own. Young turtles, if given the proper care, adjust better to captivity than do adults.

of bacterial types carried on every living—and freshly dead—thing. It is one of the common causes of stomach aches from bad potato salad at picnics and from improperly cooked chicken. Canada followed suit shortly, and today there continue in force federal laws that prohibit the sale of all aquatic turtles under 4 inches (10 cm) in shell length.

Whether these laws are realistic or not is not a question here, because they generally are adhered to, and young turtles are not legally obtainable in the United States unless you collect your own (which is not difficult to do) or swap one with a friend. In some areas the laws are openly ignored and baby Red-ears and other turtles are sold, but the ownership and display of these babies is subject to legal action if anyone complains. The states and federal government do occasionally charge pet shops with violations of the salmonella laws.

These laws have never concerned the shipment of baby turtles to other countries, and even today a good trade in baby Red-ears exists between the southern states of the United States and Japan and various other countries. However, many countries currently are trying to restrict or prohibit keeping sliders and cooters, so this may change in the near future. Incidentally, there is no practical way to ensure that a baby turtle does not carry salmonella bacteria, though the infection rate can be greatly reduced at the point of sale.

Humans, cats, dogs, hamsters, backyard birds, and even crickets carry salmonella bacteria of various types by the way, and they are generally considered harmless unless transferred to the mouth of a child with sloppy personal hygiene (which, I guess, describes most young children).

The Aquarium

Though sliders and their relatives start out as inch-long, round babies with a low keel down the center of the shell, they grow rapidly under good conditions and can reach 4 to 6 inches (10 to 15 cm) in as many years. They also are phenomenally dirty turtles. Give them the largest aquarium you can afford (nothing under 20 gallons) and equip it with both an undergravel filter and a power filter. (Your pet shop people can help you choose the proper filters and other equipment you will need.) They like warm water of at least 75 to 80°F (24 to 27°C), so you will need one or two aquarium heaters to maintain this minimal temperature all year. Additionally, sliders and cooters must bask for several hours each morning and later afternoon, so you will need a spotlight focused on a basking platform of some type. You also will need full-spectrum fluorescent lights kept on at least 12 hours a day.

The substrate should be kept simple or not used at all, because sliders constantly dig it up and put extra stress on the filters. Don't even try to keep plants in the tank, unless they are soft aquatic plants such as elodea and coontail, which most sliders find to be excellent food. You should change the entire contents of the aquarium at least weekly, because no filter is sufficient to really keep the water clean enough. Dirty tank water is brown and stinks, and you won't be able to ignore it for long. Turtles kept in dirty water usually develop shell rot (a bacterial infection) that disfigures the shell and may cause death.

substituting full-spectrum lights) in the presence of vitamin D3 to deposit calcium in the turtle's shell. If any portion of the equation—light, vitamin, calcium—is lacking, the turtle will stop growing, become soft-shelled, and die or at least become greatly deformed and stunted. YOU MUST GIVE BABY TURTLES ALL THREE PARTS OF THE EQUATION. NO EXCEPTIONS.

Today's keepers are lucky

PHOTO: W. P. MARA.

This hatchling River Cooter, *Pseudemys concinna*, nicely displays the egg tooth, the white projection from the tip of the jaws. This will be lost in a few days.

Supplements

If you keep young turtles (under 4 inches shell length), they must have supplements of digestible calcium and also of vitamin D3. There is a complex biological cycle in young turtles that involves the action of sunlight (here you are

because the proper vitamin and mineral supplements are readily available at your local pet shop. The calcium supplements today are excellent, and the vitamins are actually designed for turtles and not for hamsters or canaries. Buy the supplements, read all the directions carefully, and follow everything to the letter. Don't stint on lighting either. The proper lights may be somewhat expensive to purchase and replace regularly, but you have to do it unless you can put the turtle in an outdoor pond.

Food

As a general rule, young sliders and cooters are more carnivorous than adults. Large adults, especially females, may eat mostly vegetation, only occasionally chomping down on a snail or crayfish. There still seems to be a lot of uncertainty about just how much plant matter babies need and how much animal matter adults need. Many hobbyists get around the problem by always offering both types of food at all times, at least until they can see a trend in what the turtle accepts.

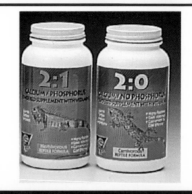

Calcium supplements are essential for the health of all young aquatic turtles. Gut-load all insect foods fed and also add calcium to the vegetables. Photo courtesy of Ocean Nutrition.

Actually, most sliders and cooters in the aquarium are omnivores and will take anything. Do not let them get hooked on Goldfish, however, which by itself seems to be deficient in some nutrients the turtles need; a continuous diet of Goldfish with just a few veggies added usually leads to deformed turtles.

Today's turtle keepers are lucky because there now are good commercial turtle diets available. These often are based on formulas for monkey chow and trout chow, and are pellets or sticks that do not fall apart in the water. Not only are the commercially prepared foods a balanced diet, they make the water easier to clean after feeding. By all means try a commercial turtle food first before digging around for earthworms, minnows, and masses of elodea. The natural foods make excellent treats to prevent boredom, however, as they give the turtles something to chase or destroy.

Processed turtle foods contain many of the nutrients needed by aquatic turtles to maintain a healthy, active life. Photo courtesy of Wardley.

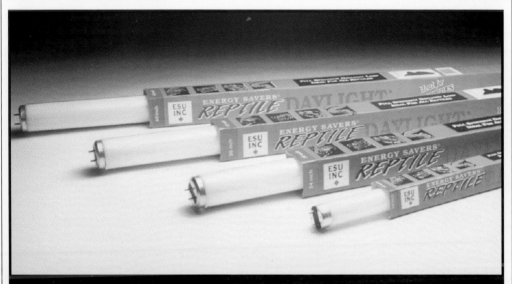

To properly convert calcium, baby turtles need sunlight or a good equivalent. Use only full-spectrum fluorescent bulbs that are designed for use with reptiles. Photo courtesy of Coralife/Energy Savers.

Illness

If you properly feed a slider, keep the water clean at all times, and provide sufficient supplements, while allowing it to bask properly at the correct water and air temperatures, you will have a healthy turtle. Almost all illnesses of water turtles are due to poor keeping practices, such as lack of vitamin A (swollen eyelids), dirty water (shell rot), or soft-shell (lack of calcium, vitamins, and proper basking and sunlight simulation). If anything untoward happens, such as parasitic infections or certain respiratory diseases, you will need the help of a veterinarian. Be sure you contact the vet at the first sign of trouble. You wouldn't expect a mechanic to keep your car running if you didn't change the oil for three or four years, so don't expect a vet to bring a turtle back from the edge of the grave.

These turtles are not short-lived animals, so death of your turtle at an age of one to two years is YOUR fault—any slider should live at least 15 years if given proper care, and some probably will live well past the 20-year mark.

Hatching of a Red-eared Slider, *Trachemys scripta elegans.*

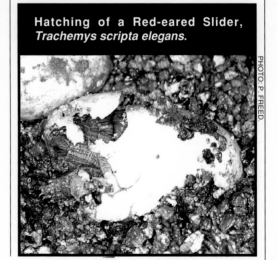

PHOTO: P. FREED

THE INCREDIBLE PAINTS

The Painted Turtle, *Chrysemys picta*, is one of the most beautiful turtles in North America and has many unique traits. If it were an import from Thailand or South Africa, collectors would be standing in line waiting to buy it, but as a native American species it has few takers.

RECOGNITION

Paints are the only common basking turtles in much of northern North America, certainly from the latitude of Pennsylvania and Iowa north. It is a relatively flat-shelled species with a black or dark olive carapace that has reddish tints on the marginals. The plastron is yellow, with or without spots, and the head has a bright yellow pattern. The back edge of the carapace is smooth, unlike the serrated or notched edge in most other related turtles. Adults typically are 4 to 6 inches (10 to 15 cm) in shell length, the females significantly larger than the males.

The upper jaw is notched at the center with a sharp cusp on each side.

This is one of the more variable American turtles, and four fairly distinct subspecies are recognized, though they intergrade broadly wherever their ranges come into contact. The Paint of the northeastern coast from Canada to North Carolina and then inland over Virginia to northern Georgia is the most distinctive subspecies because it has the edges of the costal and vertebral scutes aligned and marked with broad olive stripes. The head has two bright yellow spots (easily visible through murky water in swimming specimens), and the plastron is unmarked bright yellow, contrasting with a bright red carapace rim. This subspecies, *Chrysemys picta picta*, intergrades broadly with the subspecies of the Midwest, *C. p. marginata*, which ranges from the Great Lakes region of Canada south to Tennessee and

PHOTO: I. FRANCAIS.

Though often neglected by hobbyists, Painted Turtles (here *Chrysemys picta belli*) are beautiful animals that are not hard to keep if maintained in clean water.

PHOTO: A. NORMAN.

The bright red stripe down the center of the carapace makes the Southern Painted Turtle, *C. p. dorsalis*, one of the most desirable forms in the genus.

northern Alabama. In this subspecies (and both others as well) the costal and vertebral scutes alternate as in normal turtles. Though the colors of the head and shell are similar to *C. p. picta*, in typical *C. p. marginata* there is a large dark figure covering most of the plastron.

The subspecies *C. p. dorsalis* of the lower Mississippi Valley (from the Oklahoma-Texas border to Alabama, with lots of gaps in this range) is more domed than the northern forms and has a wide, bright orange-red or yellow middorsal stripe over the shell and an unmarked plastron. For many years this was one of the most common baby turtles in the pet hobby, but today it is not often seen because of health laws prohibiting sale of small turtles. *C. p. belli* has a tremendous range covering all the upper Great Plains into southern Canada and extending westward to Oregon and Washington plus adjacent Canada; it also exists as relict populations from an even larger range, occurring in New Mexico, Utah, and even

PHOTO: A. NORMAN.

The flattened shell, large spots behind the eye, and brown seam lines on the shell distinguish *C. p. picta*, often called the Eastern Painted Turtle.

Chihuahua, Mexico. Adults average about an inch (2.5 cm) longer than most other Paints and have the carapace covered with narrow yellowish lines that may the restricted to just the front of the scutes or form a network.

NATURAL HISTORY

The subspecies have basically similar life histories except for factors such as activity periods and incubation times that would be affected by the northern climates to which some Paints have adapted. Paints emerge from hibernation early in spring, usually by March, and are active until at least October, though specimens from the northern edge of the range come out later and go back into the mud earlier, while southern specimens may be active above the water all year. Paints are extremely resistant to cold, and they are the only higher vertebrates (i.e., anything more evolved that a fish) that can be completely frozen for several hours and then have a chance of thawing and surviving. Most Paints dig into the soft bottoms of their

Western Painted Turtles, *C. p. belli*, are very adaptable turtles than can tolerate extremes of the weather. Notice the broken yellow stripes on the carapace typical of the subspecies.

ponds, lakes, or marshes when the water temperature drops below about 68°F (20°C) for several days in a row and don't come back up until the water warms back to at least 65°F (18°C).

Paints are great baskers, often basking for hours at a time early in the day to bring up the body temperature to about 78°F (25.5°C) so they can digest food.

graduate students for almost half a century, and literally dozens of papers have been published that cover almost every aspect of the lives of the species, especially the forms that live in the northeastern United States. To try to summarize this information would take several pages and probably wouldn't help you keep Paints anyway.

PHOTO: W. P. MARA.

Hatchlings of *C. p. dorsalis* can no longer be legally sold, but many are exchanged among collectors.

They are not shy when basking, often allowing close approach, and may bask in groups of dozens of animals spread over a large log, often lying on top of each other.

If you are interested in details of the metabolism and activity patterns of turtles, then the Painted Turtle is the species for you. It has been a favorite of

BREEDING

Northern Painted Turtles are slow-growing animals that may take several years to reach sexual maturity. Males, for instance, may be four or five years old when they reach plastron lengths between 3 and 4 inches (7.5 and 10 cm) and sexual maturity, while females mature at plastron lengths between 4 and 5 inches (10 and

12.5 cm) at an age of between six and ten years. Southern Paints, which commonly do not hibernate, mature at the same lengths but an earlier age because they grow faster.

Male Painted Turtles have long, thick tails, a concave posterior plastron, and extremely long claws on their front legs. They swim after a potential mate and eventually swim past her to orient (the actual range being one to 23), depending on the size of the female and her subspecies (the large *C. p. belli* has been recorded laying the clutch of 23 eggs). Most females lay two or three clutches per year, one explanation for the abundance of Painted Turtles almost everywhere they occur. Some females lay only every second or third year, however.

PHOTO: W. P. MARA.

Baby Eastern Painted Turtles, *C. p. picta*, grow slowly from the tiny, almost round hatchlings. Even large adults, however, seldom are more than 5 inches (12.5 cm) long.

face to face. At that point the male strokes the female's face and neck with his claws, and if she is receptive to mating the female strokes his front legs in return. The female follows the male for a while and then drops to the bottom, where mating occurs.

Most nesting occurs from late May to July, a female laying anywhere from four to 15 eggs

Incubation last about two to three months over most of the range. At the northern edge of the range, where the growing season is very short, winter and freezing temperatures may occur before the young are able to leave the nest. In such cases the hatchlings overwinter in the nest, sometimes freezing for short periods. Such

An adult Southern Painted Turtle, *C. p. dorsalis*. Few adults seem to be available commercially today.

overwintering leads to very high mortalities among the hatchlings but apparently sufficient young survive to be advantageous to the species.

The young are rounded, very brightly colored turtles about an inch (2.5 cm) in diameter and bearing a distinct keel that soon becomes indistinct. They feed heavily on small invertebrates of all types, from insects and small crayfish and isopods to snails and water fleas. As they grow they become even more omnivorous, adding water plants of all types to the diet. Adults may literally eat almost anything in their pond, from elodea and waterlily flowers to dead fish and water fleas.

Paints in the North grow about an inch or more (3 cm) per year for the first three or four years, while those in the South and West grow even faster. Remember that sexual maturity in the Paints is based on size, not age. Painted Turtles from the southern part of the range probably live over 20 years, while those from the far northern portions might live over 40 years (much of this, of course, inactive in hibernation).

KEEPING

Painted Turtles are among the easiest of turtles to maintain, though like other

Painted Turtles offered for sale as adults (like these Southern Paints) usually are kept in very shallow water to make cleaning easier. They of course need to be transferred to a large aquarium or pond when you get them home.

PHOTO: M. AND J. WALLS.

PHOTO: M. PANZELLA.

These hatchlings of *C. p. picta* have a long life ahead of them if they are correctly housed and fed. Notice the two large spots behind the eyes typical of this subspecies.

aquatic species they are dirty feeders and need heavy filtration to keep their water from fouling and smelling. Dirty water may also lead to shell rot, though the rather solid shells of Paints seldom erode badly. Captives usually adapt well, especially when adult, though they will spend a lot of time trying to get out of the aquarium. They will eat almost any type of plant and animal food. No one captive-breeds this species because there is no demand for them in the market, but they should be easy to breed in greenhouses and ponds. Ponds, of course, would have to be fenced to prevent wandering and would have to be deep enough to prevent hibernation temperatures from dropping below freezing too long each year.

Hatchling Paints are delicate turtles, like the young of all the emydids. Though they are colorful, they have all the usual problems associated with young turtles, including a need for full-spectrum lighting in association with large amounts of calcium and the potential for carrying salmonellosis.

As mentioned, the brightly striped southern subspecies, *C. p. dorsalis*, once was an extremely common turtle in the pet trade, and it still appears on

PHOTO: M. PANZELLA.

PHOTO: W. P. MARA.

In Eastern Painted Turtles, *C. p. picta*, the brown edges of the costal scutes almost line up with the edges of the vertebral scutes that run over the backbone.

Left: The plastron of this baby Southern Painted Turtle, *C. p. dorsalis*, shows only a few markings that may fade even more as it grows up.

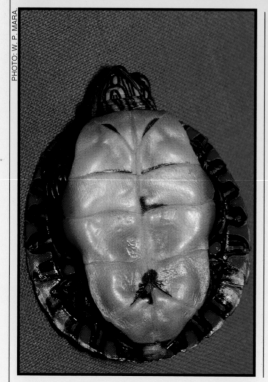

occasion. Few adults or any specimens over the legal 4 inches in carapace length are available, however, and few keepers have much luck raising young to adulthood. With today's advanced lighting systems and balanced calcium and vitamin supplements, hobbyists may have more luck raising young that they collect themselves or obtain (legally) from friends.

PHOTO: I. FRANCAIS COURTESY FISH & PET TOWN.

Portrait of an Eastern Painted Turtle, *C. p. picta*.

COOTERS

Though seven species are currently recognized in the genus *Pseudemys*, only four are though of as "real" cooters (subgenus *Pseudemys*), the rest being red-bellied turtles (subgenus *Ptychemys*). The relationships of the cooters are very complex and not totally understood, and over large parts of the United States it is impossible to accurately identify specimens because of variation and hybrid-ization. Several different concepts of relationships and subspecies have been proposed by various workers over the last 50 years, so I'll follow a more or less middle of the road course here. Changes in the names and composition of the species should be expected.

The name cooter seems to be derived from an African word, *kuta*, in general use for a freshwater turtle. The term owes its origin to African slaves brought to the southern United States in earlier centuries.

The true cooters can be distinguished by looking at the shape of the jaws. Red-bellied turtles have the center of the upper jaw deeply notched and flanked by a projecting tooth-like cusp on each side. In cooters the upper jaw is unnotched or barely notched and there is no projecting cusp on each side. Color pattern cannot be used to separate these two groups with certainty. The four species presently recognized can be separated (though not always) by color patterns of the shell.

PHOTO: M. & J. WALLS.

This large female River Cooter, *Pseudemys concinna concinna*, shows the typical black head skin and narrow yellowish (almost white) lines typical of the form.

RIVER COOTER

River Cooters, *Pseudemys concinna*, are big turtles, females often exceeding 16 inches (40 cm) in length. The back of the shell often is flared and is serrated.

Though adults tend to be just big, blackish turtles, there usually are traces of pattern on the costals that can be seen if the turtle is submerged in water. The second costal scute has at least traces of a large, backwardly facing C on the posterior half, the result of the yellow background color showing through where several irregular dark whorls fail to overlap. The plastron is yellow with at least traces of pattern anteriorly and often with a parallel pattern of lines and ovals along the seams; there usually are at least two or three pairs of dark ovals present on the front third of the plastron even in fairly large adults. The skin is blackish with narrow yellow lines on the legs and face.

About five subspecies of River Cooter are recognized, but it is doubtful if most of these can be

PHOTO: DR. P. C. H. PRITCHARD

The Peninsula Cooter, *P. [floridana] peninsularis*, of Florida shows the vertical striping on the second costal scute that is typical of cooters other than the River Cooter.

recognized in the hand, let alone in the field. *P. c. concinna* is found along the southeastern coast from Virginia to central Georgia; *P. c. hieroglyphica* is a form of western Tennessee to northern Alabama and Mississippi; the doubtful *P. c. mobilensis* is from

If you look hard, you can just make out the reversed C on the second costal scute that helps identify the River Cooter. Notice the leech at the edge of the shell.

PHOTO: M. & J. WALLS

the Gulf Coast; *P. c. suwanniensis* is restricted to large rivers along the northwestern coast of Florida; and *P. c. metteri* is found from southwestern Missouri to central Oklahoma and southeastern Texas. Supposedly every River Cooter from Louisiana to western Georgia is an intergrade between two or more subspecies. Rely on a good field guide for detailed identification. There are no River Cooters in most of peninsular Florida.

PHOTO: DR. P. C. H. PRITCHARD.

This young River Cooter belongs to the form or subspecies from the Gulf Coast that once was called *P. floridana hoyi*, today a synonym of *P. c. concinna*. The taxonomy of these turtles remains unsettled.

A recently published paper by Michael Seidel, who long has studied the cooters, comes to the conclusion that all the normally recognized subspecies but *suwanniensis* are invalid, and the very dark *suwanniensis* itself represents a full species. This view would certainly make the River Cooter easier to understand, but it is likely to be contested by other workers.

Hatchling and young River Cooters are pretty turtles, bright yellow with many green and black whorls like fingerprints over the carapace. They used to be common in the pet trade and still occur on occasion. Look for a distinct dark plastral pattern to be sure of identification once you've checked for the absence of cusps on the upper jaw.

River Cooters are very aquatic turtles that seldom venture onto land except to nest. They prefer deeper water and can spend more than two hours submerged. They feed mostly on aquatic vegetation, though young and even adults also take snails, aquatic insects, crustaceans, and occasionally fishes. They also scavenge on dead animals washed into the water. Feeding occurs early and late in the day, with the hours between spent basking.

Like other North American cooters and sliders, male River Cooters have long claws on the front feet that they wave or vibrate in the female's face before settling to the bottom to mate. Males also may hover over the female while stroking her face from above. Females lay about 10 to 20 eggs in a nest with three openings, a central true nest and two false nests to the sides. They may even put an egg or two in each false nest. Most nests still are destroyed by crows and raccoons, however. Hatching takes about three months. Hatchlings are high-domed and about 1 to 1.5 inches (2.5 to 3.5 cm) long, with bright colors. They sometimes spend the winter in the nest if hatching occurs too late in the season to come out and feed before having to hibernate. The young grow fast until they become sexually mature

PHOTO: W. P. MARA.

Freaks or sports often occur in baby turtles. This very interesting specimen appears to be a River Cooter in which most of the color on the body and shell is missing. If it matures and breeds, it might produce attractive offspring.

at about four years in males and six years or more in females. There is a longevity record of over 40 years for this species.

PHOTO: R. D. BARTLETT.

The hatchling Florida Cooter, P. [c.] floridana, is a beautiful little turtle. Notice that the second costal scute has a vertical yellow line, not a C.

Captive care is much as in the Red-ear, but you have to allow for the much larger size of the average adult. Because they like deep water, you probably will need a very large aquarium if you wish the animals to mature without stunting or distortion.

RIO GRANDE COOTER

In the lower Rio Grande drainage of Texas and adjacent Mexico and the Pecos drainage of western Texas and New Mexico is found a dark cooter that is very closely related to the River Cooter but is isolated from it by over a hundred miles. This is *Pseudemys gorzugi*, a somewhat doubtful species that has the flared, serrated posterior shell of the River Cooter and the yellow plastron marked with dark as in that species, but the second costal has five distinct whorls (in young and half-grown specimens) of black and greenish separated by the yellow background color (only four whorls in the River Cooter). The stripe behind the eye is interrupted to produce a fairly large yellow spot (usually not so in the River Cooter). Otherwise the two species are very similar.

Several years ago I happened to be driving through southern Texas north of Brownsville following exceptionally heavy June rains. The interstate highway was littered

A hatchling Suwannee Cooter, P. [concinna] suwanniensis, shows the bright pattern of most young River Cooters. Notice the open C on the second costal scute.

PHOTO: R. D. BARTLETT.

A baby River Cooter, *P. concinna concinna*.

PHOTO: A. NORMAN.

for several miles with living and dead Rio Grande Cooters killed by traffic while they were moving from the deep water-filled ditches on each side of the highway. All were large (the maximum size for this species is about 9 inches or 23 cm, but some of these turtles certainly were larger), very dark females with almost no visible pattern on the shell and only traces of a head pattern. The dead ones were serving as a feast for Caracaras, a large, beautiful bird of prey related to the falcons that often feeds on carrion. Very few of the turtles must have been able to make it across to road to successfully nest.

Rains are few and sometimes far between in much of the area inhabited by the Rio Grande Cooter, and it should be expected that specimens can cope with long periods when no surface water is available.

COOTER

Along the coast of the southeastern United States from the Virginia border to about Mobile Bay is found the "true" Cooter, *Pseudemys floridana*. This is the common cooter of the Florida peninsula, a big (16 inches, 40 cm, in large females), dark, very high-domed and thick-shelled species that can be recognized by the combination of lack of cusps on the upper jaw (there is no central notch either), a yellow plastron that is totally lacking in dark markings, and (when visible) a wide yellow vertical bar on the second costal

The Rio Grande Slider, *P. gorzugi*, has a more complicated shell pattern than the River Cooter, but often the pattern is broken or difficult to see in adults. This is one of the most poorly understood North American turtles.

PHOTO: R. D. BARTLETT.

PHOTO: R. D. BARTLETT.

Look hard and you will see the yellow "hairpin" behind the eye of this Peninsula Cooter, *P. [floridana] peninsularis*. Formed by the joining of two lines that are separate in most other cooters, it is one of the many distinctive features of this turtle.

scute. Two subspecies are recognized: *P. f. floridana* over all the range but peninsular Florida has many narrow yellow stripes on top of the head, none joined, while *P. f. peninsularis* of the peninsula has some of the stripes joined to form narrow curved "hairpins" on each side of the head. Juveniles are dark green and yellow, the carapace covered with uneven greenish, mostly vertical bars and lines on a yellow ground color, unlike the "fingerprint" whorls of the River Cooter.

This is somewhat more of a pond and lake species than the River Cooter, liking soft bottoms and abundant vegetation. It spends much of the day basking, feeding on vegetation early and late in the day. Often groups of dozens of turtles are seen basking at a preferred spot, stacked on top of each other. They bask with other species without any aggressive interaction. Unlike the River Cooter, true Cooters often leave the water and wander about on land even when not nesting.

Males have the long front claws expected in North American cooters and sliders, using them to entice the female in a face-to-face courtship display. Females lay clutches of about 20 eggs two or more times per year. In central and southern Florida the turtles may lay at any time of the year, but in the rest of the range nesting tends to occur between May and July. At the northern edge of the range, hatchlings may spend the winter in the nest. Like the River Cooter, and unlike any other related species as far as known (the Rio Grande Cooter seems to remain unknown), the true Cooter digs a nest with a

PHOTO: R. D. BARTLETT.

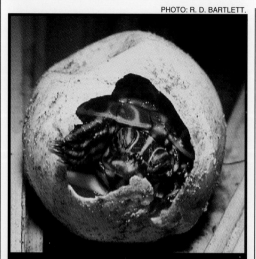

Hatching of the Peninsula Cooter, P. [floridana] peninsularis.

deep central cavity and two false nests to the sides. Incubation lasts about 75 to 150 days, probably averaging closer to 75 in southern Florida. Males in South Carolina reach maturity in about three years at a plastron length of 4 to 5 inches (10 to 12 cm), while females can produce eggs only after they reach 8 to 9.5 inches (20 to 24 cm) in length in probably their sixth or seventh year.

The relationships of the cooters, as mentioned earlier, are very complex. I personally have a lot of trouble recognizing the "key character" of a open C on the second costal in *P. concinna* and a vertical bar in *P. floridana*. Where the two species occur together they often hybridize, producing populations with mostly intermediate individuals. An additional complication is that in western Florida the River Cooter often develops a reddish tint on the plastron and edge of the carapace and may even have small cusps on either side of the central notch of the upper jaw, resembling the Florida Red-belly to some extent. There remains much basic taxonomic work to be done on these common and easily observed turtles.

Because *P. floridana* hybridizes so often with *P. concinna*, Michael Seidel has recently combined the two into a single species as *P. c. concinna* and *P. c. floridana*. He also recognizes as a full species *P. peninsularis* from most of Florida. If his ideas are accepted, the southeastern cooters would consist of three species with just four subspecies: *P. c. concina*, *P. c. floridana*, *P. suwanniensis*, and

The dark green hatchlings (notice the egg tooth) of *P. [floridana] peninsularis* are a familiar sight in southern Florida, where this is the only cooter.

PHOTO: P. FREED.

P. peninsularis. Of course, it may be ten years or more before his classification is generally accepted.

TEXAS RIVER COOTER

Pseudemys texana is an odd species that formerly was considered to be a subspecies of *P. concinna.* It ranges widely in the rivers of central and south-central Texas and is green and black "fingerprint" whorls on a yellow background like the River Cooter and there is only an indication of the arrow on top of the head that marks the true red-bellies. It is known that River Cooters in western Florida sometimes develop red plastra and notched and cusped upper jaws, and a similar type of development from *P. concinna*

PHOTO: R. D. BARTLETT.

A baby Florida Cooter, *P. [concinna] floridana.* The high-domed carapace is normal. Notice that the lines behind the eyes are separate, not joined into a hairpin. Whether this turtle is a full species or a subspecies of *P. concinna* remains controversial.

apparently not in contact with *P. concinna* to the north and *P. gorzugi* to the south. Though the upper jaw is notched and has strong cusps like the red-bellies and there is a tendency for some specimens to have red-rimmed plastra, the carapace pattern consists of may mark the origin of the Texas River Cooter. The yellow to white head pattern is very variable, but usually it comprises at least a broad stripe behind the eye and a vertical bar behind the angle of the jaws. Adult males are about 10 inches (25 cm) long

PHOTO: R. D. BARTLETT.

Though the shell shape and pattern of the Texas River Cooter, *P. texana*, closely match those of *P. concinna*, the two are considered full species because they have separate ranges and do not intergrade.

and have rather flattened carapaces that flare posteriorly and are deeply notched; females are larger and more domed.

The very broken head pattern of the Texas River Cooter is unique in the genus, and no two specimens match exactly.

PHOTO: R. D. BARTLETT.

Males have the usual long claws on the front toes, and it is assumed that courtship proceeds as in other North American *Pseudemys*. It seems (on limited evidence) that males mature in three years and females in six. Females lay clutches of about 10 to 15 eggs in May and June; it is not known if more than one clutch is laid. The eggs hatch in August and September, an incubation period of about three months.

Though widely distributed and common, the Texas River Cooter, because of taxonomic confusion, remains one of the least understood North American turtles.

RED-BELLIES

The species of *Pseudemys* with deep notches at the center of the upper jaw flanked by strong tooth-like cusps are placed in the subgenus *Ptychemys*. They also as a rule have very rugose (wrinkled) carapace scutes in adults, a reddish plastron (sometimes just the rim) and often carapace, and a yellow arrow between the eyes ending on the snout. These are the red-bellied turtles, some of the most attractive North American species with many fans in the pet hobby.

Only three species of red-bellies are recognized, each separated geographically along the eastern coast of the United States from Massachusetts to Alabama. These species are very similar and almost certainly represent relicts of a single, once more wide-ranging species that died back over much of the range perhaps a million or more years ago and left isolated populations that evolved into the present three species (which have been treated as subspecies by some authors). *Pseudemys texana* sometimes is added to the group but is found only in central and eastern Texas. Other than the notching and cusping of the upper jaw, it has little resemblance to the eastern red-bellies and instead looks much like a form of the River Cooter, with which it long was associated.

NORTHERN RED-BELLIED TURTLE

From southern New Jersey south along the coast to northeastern North Carolina is found the large (females to 16 inches, 40 cm), high-shelled, very dark *Pseudemys rubriventris*. This species was described more than a century and half ago from the Delaware River near Trenton, and it still occurs there today, though far from conspicuous. It is a species of rivers and lakes as well as large ponds and marshes, and it often basks along with Painted Turtles. It fits the description of the subgenus well, having strong cusps alongside the median notch in the upper jaw, a distinct yellow arrow on top of the head, and a red plastron, marginals, and vertical bars on the

PHOTO BY R.D. BARLETT.

A well-marked young Northern Red-bellied Turtle, *Pseudemys rubriventris*, from Maryland.

costal scutes. Juveniles are much more colorful than the dark adults, being greenish with bright red or deep orange markings on the shell. *P. rubriventris* is very closely related to the Florida Red-belly (*P. nelsoni*), differing mostly in having more yellow lines on the face (5) and more dark pattern on the plastron of hatchlings; the species are best identified by locality.

Though found in a heavily populated and well-studied area, little is known about the breeding biology of this species. The male has long claws on the front feet and assumedly uses them to stroke the face of the female before mating. Nesting takes place in May and June, the female laying clutches of about six to

PHOTO: K. T. NEMURAS.

Baby Northern Red-bellies, *P. rubriventris*, like this one have bright red plastrons and a large amount of black pattern along the seams. In the Forida Red-belly the black is restricted to a few large spots.

12 eggs once or twice per year. Incubation takes two to three months, and young from the second clutch may have to hibernate in the nest. The

An adult Northern Red-bellied Turtle, *P. rubriventris*, from southern New Jersey. This is a very dark or melanistic specimen in which little of the shell or head pattern is visible.

PHOTO: M. PANZELLA.

turtle seems to be slow to mature (males have been stated to mature at about 9 inches plastron length at an age of nine years), but the figures given seem somewhat off compared to related species and there still is much to be learned. Like other *Pseudemys*, adults feed mostly on aquatic vegetation but juveniles take more invertebrates. Adults are not attracted to dead fish but will take fish in captivity. The species has not fared well in captivity, seldom living more than a few years.

A few hundred Northern Red-bellies isolated in ponds in southeastern Massachusetts have long been distinguished as a separate subspecies, *P. r. bangsi*, but repeated modern studies of this form have failed to find any characters to distinguish it from more southerly members of the species. There are subfossil specimens of the Massachusetts Red-belly, so if it represents an introduced population it must have been introduced by Amerindians a long time ago. Massachusetts populations are protected by federal law.

FLORIDA RED-BELLIED TURTLE

In almost all respects *Pseudemys nelsoni* is a southern form of *P. rubriventris*, differing mostly in having a brighter color in many specimens and less dark patterning on the plastron of juveniles. The yellow stripes on the head are reduced in number (3) and sometimes partially fused. The species is confined to Florida except for extending a short way into adjacent Georgia, and it is most abundant in the peninsula.

Though adult Florida Red-bellied Turtles, *P. nelsoni*, often have rough, eroded shells, most specimen show broad vertical reddish bars over the costal scutes.

PHOTO: A. NORMAN.

Adult females reach at least 15 inches (38 cm) in shell length, males being smaller. Often both sexes are heavily covered with black pigment that obscures the red, but turtles in the water almost always have some red visible on the marginals or costals.

Males reach sexual maturity at a plastron length of 7 to 8 inches (17 to 20 cm) and an age of about three years, while females don't mature until at least five years old and over 10 inches (26 cm) long. Courtship and nesting are as in other *Pseudemys*, females laying a dozen or more eggs as often as five or six times per year. The female often digs her nests in alligator nests. Incubation takes about two months, producing brilliantly colored hatchlings a bit over an inch (2.8 cm) long. Adults feed almost exclusively on aquatic plants, while young take more aquatic insects, snails, and crustaceans.

ALABAMA RED-BELLIED TURTLE

Restricted to the rivers and streams around Mobile Bay in southern Alabama, *Pseudemys alabamensis* long has been a rare and poorly understood turtle. The carapace is very deep and rugose. The yellow stripes on either side of the arrow on top of the head are long, extending froward over or beyond the eyes (they stop behind the eyes in the Florida Red-belly). The red of the pattern may be reduced and more yellowish than reddish, and the plastron is yellowish red and has a rather

Pseudemys alabamensis, the Alabama Red-bellied Turtle, is a declining species with a very limited range in southern Alabama.

PHOTO: R. D. BARTLETT.

PHOTO: R. D. BARTLETT.

At first glance—and even second glance—*P. alabamensis* looks almost exactly like *P. nelsoni*. Range is the best way to distinguish these sibling (sister) species.

strong dark pattern in young specimens. Again, the species is best identified by locality.

Alabama Red-bellies have only recently been studied in any detail. They live in areas with dense aquatic vegetation and may be active all year during mild winters. They bask like related turtles but seem to be shy and easily disturbed. Adult females reach at least 13 inches (33 cm) in length, the males smaller. Males have elongated front claws, females lay about 18 eggs per clutch, and the eggs hatch in about two months. Most females of the species once nested on a single island, but today almost none of the nests escape predation from crows, raccoons, and (sometimes) man. The species is protected by federal law but probably cannot survive much longer. It has survived in captivity for over ten years.

The only reason this form is considered a distinct species is because it presently does not come into contact with the Florida Red-belly. There is fossil evidence to show that the Florida Red-belly once extended north to South Carolina, and the recent discovery of an apparently undescribed red-bellied turtle to the northwest of the range of *P. alabamensis* ties in well with the idea that the red-bellies all are part of what was until recently one continuous species.

NORTHERN SLIDERS

Sliders are the most familiar turtles in the hobby, even though their general sale has been restricted for over 20 years. One subspecies, the Red-eared Slider, takes most of the glory—or the risks, as you prefer—in the trade, with thousands or hundreds of thousands being shipped from the southern United States around the world.

The genus of the sliders, *Trachemys*, is perhaps the most complicated of the group we are discussing here. The species fall into three fairly distinct groups geographically: 1) those of the United States, including the lower Rio Grande drainage and adjacent Mexico; 2) forms of tropical America from Uruguay and Brazil north through Central America to northern Mexico and the upper Rio Grande drainage of Texas and New Mexico; 3) those of the Caribbean islands. Traditionally all the forms of the American mainland have been considered subspecies of *T. scripta*, the species found in the United States, even though many of the 16 or so described subspecies are allopatric (meaning that their ranges do not come into contact so they have no opportunity to intergrade if they really are subspecies). By contrast, the sliders of the Caribbean are considered full species even though they overlap considerably in characters (without intergrading) yet are found on separate islands.

Because there are two major distinctions between the sliders of North America and those of tropical America, I am going to use these groups as distinct species for the moment, using the name *Trachemys scripta* for the northern species that has a short, rather blunt snout and long foreclaws in males, and the names *T. ornata* and *T. dorbigni* for the two tropical American species with more or

PHOTO: R. D. BARTLETT.

Detail of the head pattern of a Northern Slider, *Trachemys scripta scripta*, often called the Yellow-bellied Slider. The exact shape of the yellow blotch varies considerably.

less projecting to bulbous snouts and short foreclaws in males. *T. ornata* is the oldest name for all the described tropical forms from northern Mexico and the upper Rio Grande south through Venezuela, and it is used for convenience until a researcher has the nerve to officially split the tropical forms into the dozen or so full species that probably should be recognized.

subspecies and not species. Though they usually just go by the common name of Slider, this seems inappropriately simple considering the complexity of the group, and I prefer to call them the Northern Slider. As a general rule I don't like to use formal common names for subspecies, but *T. scripta elegans* is so deeply entrenched in the literature, both scientific and hobbyist, as the Red-eared Slider that I am forced

PHOTO: A. NORMAN.

In this partially grown *T. scripta scripta* the yellow blotch has split into two parts, a stripe back from the eye and a vertical bar leading to the chin stripe.

RECOGNITION

The three commonly recognized subspecies of slider found in the United States, and just getting over the international border into northeastern Mexico, form a very closely knit group that intergrade where their ranges come into contact and certainly are

to go along with it.

The species *Trachemys scripta* is a moderately large turtle with a fairly low carapace. Large females may reach over 11 inches (29 cm) in shell length, but males reach only 8 inches (20 cm). The snout is rounded and not especially long, nor is it upturned or

PHOTO: K. T. NEMURAS.

The Yellow-bellied Slider, *T. scripta scripta*. This subspecies from the southeastern United States often appears in the pet trade.

bulbous even in adult males. The carapace is greenish to brownish with a vertical yellow bar on most costal scutes along with vertical and angled black lines. The posterior edge of the carapace is deeply serrated and often flared. The front legs have narrow yellow stripes, while the thighs have vertical yellow or whitish stripes somewhat like those of a Chicken Turtle. The skin in greenish to brownish, seldom glossy black, and there are several yellow stripes on the head and neck. In all three subspecies there is a broadened stripe behind the eye that may be bright yellow to bright red. The plastron is yellow, usually with pairs of black ovals (which may be reduced or absent).

Two well-marked subspecies can be recognized in the species, along with another subspecies that seems to me to be of doubtful validity. The subspecies found mostly in coastal drainages from southeastern Virginia to southern Alabama (but not in peninsular Florida) is *T. s. scripta*, readily recognized by the presence of a broad, somewhat irregular yellow blotch behind the eye in combination with a nearly or completely unmarked yellow plastron. This subspecies intergrades with the Red-eared Slider, *T. s. elegans*, over most of Alabama, producing specimens that are at least partially intermediate between the two subspecies. *T. s. elegans* has a broad stripe behind the eye that is almost always bright red in both babies and typical adults,

Ventral or plastral view of a large female Red-eared Slider, *T. s. elegans*, from Texas. Notice the heavy markings even in this 11-inch (28-cm) specimen

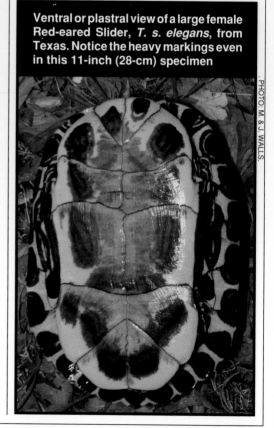

PHOTO: M & J WALLS.

especially females. Old males of this subspecies are especially prone to melanism, where the color pattern disappears under a layer of dark brown mottling; such males may have solid dark heads with no red visible behind the eye. The Red-ear is found over much of the Mississippi River basin and the lower Ohio drainage west to central Texas and into northeastern Mexico.

it resembles a stabilized intergrade between the other subspecies, and occasional workers have cast doubt on just what this subspecies represents.

NATURAL HISTORY

The life of the Northern Slider does not differ greatly from that of the cooters or even the Painted Turtle. It is a basking species found in a variety of

PHOTO: M. & J. WALLS.

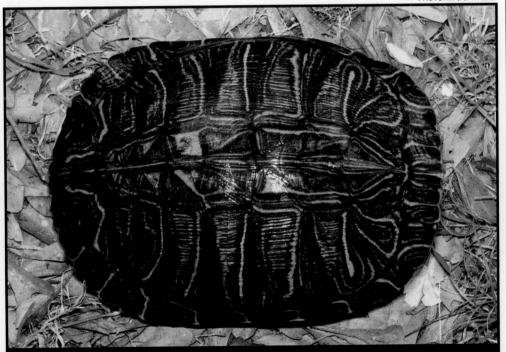

Old Red-ears often still have very distinct shell patterns. Notice the flare at the back of the shell that helps protect the hind legs.

The third subspecies, *T. s. troosti*, is restricted to the upper Cumberland and Tennessee River drainages of central Tennessee and adjacent states. It is smaller than the other subspecies, has a weakly marked plastron, and has a broad yellow stripe behind the eye. In virtually all its characters

waters though usually avoiding faster rivers and streams. It likes lakes and slow rivers with moderately deep, clean water over a soft bottom and with lots of aquatic vegetation. Basking sites, such as downed trees and mats of vegetation, are necessary, because this species spends much of its day in the sun. Northern Sliders become inactive, or at least do not feed, when water temperatures drop below 50°F (10°C) for several days in a row, but except at the northern edge of the range they do not hibernate and can be seen swimming and basking even in mid-winter in most of the South. They can stay under water for at least two or three hours before becoming stressed, but more typically they make only short dives in search of food and to escape predators. Unlike most aquatic turtles, an individual Northern Slider may call several adjacent ponds home, venturing from one to the other on a somewhat regular basis (and often not making it across the highway in the process). These sliders like to wander and sometimes can be found long distances from water. Melanistic males have several differences in physiology from normally colored males and tend to be more aggressive, often being the dominant turtles in a population.

Like related turtles, juvenile Northern Sliders are carnivores feeding on a variety of small invertebrates and vertebrates (if they can catch them). During their second year they start to become progressively more vegetarian, taking

This half-grown Red-ear nicely shows the gigantic webbed hind feet typical of all the cooters and sliders. These are very efficient swimming turtles, something to be remembered when housing a specimen.

PHOTO: I. FRANCAIS

PHOTO: R. D. BARTLETT.

Red-ears and other sliders and cooters must bask! The sunlight not only helps convert calcium into bone, but it dries the shell and helps kill bacteria and algae that could cause shell deformities. They bask even on warm days in mid-winter in the South.

a wide variety of plants, and adults feed heavily on vegetation. However, it might be more appropriate to say that this species is an omnivore, as adults take meat of all types (from snails to snakes) if they can get it. Studies even show that large adults will choose animal foods over plant foods if given a choice. They need a water temperature of at least 65°F (18°C) to begin feeding in the spring.

BREEDING

The age and size of maturity in the Northern Slider vary considerably with climate and food availability (as well as, perhaps, genetics). Males are mature at a plastron length of about 4 inches (10 cm), at which time they have the long foreclaws and long tails of their sex. Females do not mature until a plastron length of typically 7 to 9 inches (17 to 23 cm) and an age of probably closer to five years than three. The species goes through a courtship much like the species of *Chrysemys* and *Pseudemys*, the male chasing after the female and eventually outpacing her to turn face to face. The pair then do an elaborate ballet in the water, the male stroking the sides of the female's face with the backs of his claws; the female swims in place during the courtship and closes her eyes, later slowly sinking to

PHOTO: P. FREED.

The so-called pastel mutation (reduced dark pigmentation) produces some striking Red-ears, *T. s. elegans*. This specimen has the red developed on top of the head as well as behind the eye. .

good. The eggs hatch after two to three months, producing the well-known green juveniles that are about an inch (2.5 cm) in diameter. Babies commonly spend several hours in the egg before emerging completely, and at the northern edge of the range they may spend the winter in the nest. As in related turtles, the sex of a hatchling is determined by the temperatures during incubation. Males hatch from eggs kept at temperatures below about 81°F (27°C), while females develop at temperatures closer to 86°F (30°C).

the bottom as the male moves to her rear to copulate. In *T. s. scripta* the female may actively court the male, and subadults of the species may engage in a false courtship, the young male stroking a young female's face even though he has only short claws.

PHOTO: R. D. BARTLETT.

Other pastels are greener and overall just duller turtles. This baby pastel Red-ear probably would be left out of a selective breeding program.

KEEPING

The Northern Slider, especially the Red-

Nesting occurs in spring and early summer, the female often venturing far from water in search of proper nesting conditions. The goblet-shaped nest usually is less than 5 inches (12.5 cm) deep and holds six to 20 eggs. Larger females lay more eggs than smaller females, as might be expected, and a female may lay three to five clutches per year if the food and weather are

A melanistic male Red-eared Slider, *T. s. elegans*. In some parts of the South most males are nearly black. This may aid in better use of the sun's heat during basking.

PHOTO: R. D. BARTLETT.

eared subspecies, has been a mainstay of the pet industry for decades and continues even today to be produced in large quantities for shipment to Japan and other countries. I've seen estimates of up to 4 million turtles exported each year from the United States, mostly Louisiana, most of these hatchlings produced by retaining gravid females until they lay and then hatching the eggs. The young may be subjected to high doses of antibiotics to reduce the chances of salmonellosis contamination, but such treatments seldom work. Several countries, including

PHOTO: R. D. BARTLETT.

A basking young albino Red-eared Slider. Their shells often appear dirty because of algae growing on the surface.

PHOTO: M. & J. WALLS.

Head-on view of a large female Red-eared Slider. There are no distinct cusps on either side of the notch, one of the characteristics of the genus *Trachemys*.

Italy and Great Britain, currently are considering ways of restricting trade in the Red-ear and may eventually close off trade in the species entirely.

The captive care of this species has been discussed in detail by Patterson in his book *Red-eared Slider Turtles*, and I've touched on the high points in the first chapter of this book. Just remember that these are dirty turtles that need heavy filtration and regular water changes, and hatchlings and young turtles need exceptionally large amounts of calcium and vitamin D3 supplementation in combination with full-spectrum lighting.

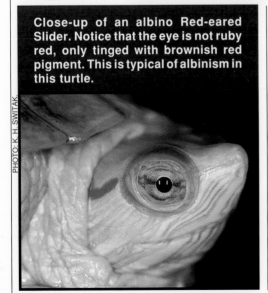

Close-up of an albino Red-eared Slider. Notice that the eye is not ruby red, only tinged with brownish red pigment. This is typical of albinism in this turtle.

PHOTO: K. H. SWITAK.

Pastel Red-ears, which seem to be a type of hypomelanistic (reduced pigmentation) mutation, recently have become available at high prices but are attractive animals well worth the extra cost and attention they require. Albinos also are available, but to me they look like rather weak turtles; additionally, their shells seem to always turn a dirty brown because of algal growth, making them lose most of their attractive features. Undoubtedly if more specimens are bred in captivity further mutations will appear to brighten up the aquarium of the determined hobbyist.

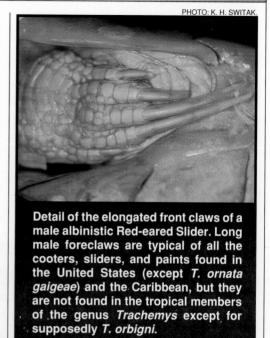

PHOTO: K. H. SWITAK.

Detail of the elongated front claws of a male albinistic Red-eared Slider. Long male foreclaws are typical of all the cooters, sliders, and paints found in the United States (except *T. ornata gaigeae*) and the Caribbean, but they are not found in the tropical members of the genus *Trachemys* except for supposedly *T. orbigni*.

This male (notice the long front claws) albino Red-eared Slider is typical of most specimens. The red ear is bright and clear, but the rest of the shell and body appear dirty pinkish.

PHOTO: K. H. SWITAK

TROPICAL SLIDERS

For purposes of discussion only, I am considering that two species of sliders are found from northern Mexico into southern South America. *Trachemys ornata*, the Tropical Slider, ranges from Venezuela north to the Mexico-United States border as a series of at least 15 isolated or partially isolated groups of populations, most of which have been given scientific names. Another species, the Brazilian Slider, *T. dorbigni*, occurs at least from Argentina and Uruguay into southern Brazil and may be more widely distributed but is poorly known. There is no doubt that *T. ornata* includes many groups that if described today would be considered full species because they are widely separated from the next closest populations.

PHOTO: R. D. BARTLETT.

The ringed pattern on the costal scutes marks the juveniles of many subspecies of the Tropical Slider. This is the nominate form, *Trachemys ornata ornata*.

TROPICAL SLIDER

The "species" here called *Trachemys ornata* cannot be defined, but as a general rule it can be distinguished from the Northern Slider, *T. scripta*, by the carapace pattern consisting of a dark spot on each costal scute, usually surrounded by a yellow or orange circle; short claws on the front feet of adult males; a tendency toward elongate, upturned, sometimes bulbous snouts in adult males; and the presence of a red or red-brown stripe or isolated spot behind the eye (often similar to that of the Red-eared Slider but equally commonly failing to reach the eye).

Biologically the Tropical Slider differs little from the Northern Slider, possibly because this species entered tropical America only recently (perhaps only a million years ago or so) and has developed small differences in color patterns and sizes without changing its biology. The egg clutches often are larger than in Northern Sliders and may develop more quickly. The Tropical Slider likes the same types of habitats as the Northern Slider, generally slow or still water with many basking areas and extensive beds of aquatic vegetation. They seldom occur where there is heavy tree cover, as in rainforests, or where there is little vegetation, but there are exceptions to both these rules. *T. ornata* ranges from the upper Rio Grande drainage in New Mexico, Texas, and northern Mexico, to northern Venezuela. The northernmost subspecies, *T. o. gaigeae*, often is recognized as a full species, the Rio Grande Slider, easily recognized by the squarish to somewhat rounded red spot behind the eye. Similarly, the two southernmost subspecies—*T. o. callirostris* in Colombia and Venezuela and *T. o. chichiriviche* in northeastern Venezuela—are isolated and distinctive in color patterns (many yellow spots on the chin and jaws in the first, a dark reddish brown pointed wedge behind the eye in the second) and could with good reason be considered full species in their own rights. Between these extreme populations are ten described subspecies (and a few

PHOTO: S. L & J. T. COLLINS.

The Big Bend Slider, *T. o. gaigeae*, is the only Tropical Slider found north into the United States. Often it is considered a full species, but it seems to be very closely related to three or four other subspecies of Tropical Sliders found in northern Mexico.

so-far unnamed ones), several of which are known to be so variable that they eventually will be broken into several more subspecies. Obviously the situation is so tangled that it confounds the experts, let alone hobbyists.

For reference sake, the described subspecies include: *gaigeae*, upper Rio Grande drainage; *taylori*, Cuatro Cienegas, Coahuila, Mexico (known to hybridize with introduced Red-eared Sliders); *hartwegi*, Rio Nazas drainage, north-central Mexico; *hiltoni*, Sonora and Sinaloa, Mexico; *nebulosa*, southern Baja California, Mexico; *yaquia*, Sonora, Mexico; *ornata*, Sinaloa, Pacific Mexico; *grayi*, extreme southern Pacific Mexico and Guatemala to El Salvador; *cataspila*, Tamaulipas, northeastern

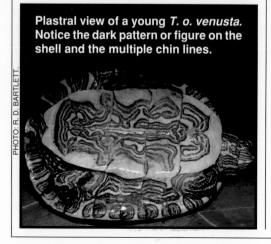

PHOTO: R. D. BARTLETT.

Plastral view of a young *T. o. venusta*. Notice the dark pattern or figure on the shell and the multiple chin lines.

PHOTO: I. FRANCAIS, COURTESY ABBOTT.

Occasionally small specimens of the Tropical Slider, *T. o. ornata*, are available, some of them captive-bred. This is one of the more attractive sliders.

Mexico (may intergrade or hybridize with the Red-eared Slider; this is the Tropical Slider that occurs closest to the Northern Slider); *venusta*, Veracruz, Mexico, south along the Atlantic lowlands of Central America to Panama and then barely into Colombia (this subspecies is certainly a complex of four or more forms); *emolli*, Costa Rica in the Lakes Nicaragua and Managua drainages; *callirostris*, Colombia and western Venezuela; *chichiriviche*, northeastern Venezuela. Hobbyists who need to identify Tropical Sliders to subspecies should consult the more technical literature.

In the middle and late 1970's large numbers of *T. o. callirostris*, then called the Venezuelan Slider, appeared on

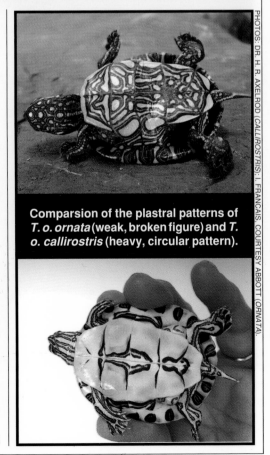

Comparsion of the plastral patterns of *T. o. ornata* (weak, broken figure) and *T. o. callirostris* (heavy, circular pattern).

PHOTOS: DR. H. R. AXELROD (CALLIROSTRIS); I. FRANCAIS, COURTESY ABBOTT (ORNATA).

Identifying the subspecies of the Tropical Slider is very difficult or impossible. They just are too poorly known to identify without detailed locality data. The young specimens above probably are *T. o. grayi*, while the adult below is the colorful *T. o. venusta* from Veracruz, Mexico. Photos: Top, J. W. Church; Bottom: Dr. P. C. H. Pritchard.

PHOTO: DR. P. C. H. PRITCHARD.

T. o. cataspila from northeastern Mexico occurs near the range of *T. scripta elegans*, and the two may hybridize where man has broken down natural barriers.

One of the most distinctive subspecies of the Tropical Slider is *T. o. chichiriviche* from northeastern Venezuela (below and top left). Notice that the broad red postorbital stripe is blocked from the eye by several narrow yellow lines and the carapace has an odd sculptured appearance. Photos: R. D. Bartlett.

PHOTO: M. FREIBERG.

The distinctive chin markings of *T. dorbigni*. This specimen belongs to the doubtful subspecies *brasiliensis*.

being banned for health reasons). Like other hatchling sliders, they needed large amounts of calcium and vitamin D3, which generally were not available at the time, and most died in a few months to a couple of years. Those that survived soon grew too large for the typical aquarium and were abandoned in local waters, where they presumably died during the first winter. I personally knew of two 6-inch (15-cm) specimens that were introduced into a lake in central Louisiana, where they must have had some

PHOTO: M. FREIBERG.

the American pet market, probably imported from Colombia (the Rio Magdalena basin of Colombia contains one of the major populations of this form and at that time was heavily collected for tropical fishes). The attractive head and chin pattern and ocellated carapace made the turtles very attractive to hobbyists, and for a few years they were literally everywhere, replacing for a time the Red-eared Slider (which was in the process of

Ventral pattern of a hatchling Brazilian Slider, *T. dorbigni brasiliensis*.

An old adult *T. dorbigni dorbigni*.

PHOTO: M. FREIBERG.

interesting competition from the local Red-ears until the first freeze of winter. Even today a few *callirostris* and the occasional other subspecies are imported in small numbers, usually as either hatchlings (definitely illegal under the 4-inch salmonella laws) or large adults (which might be easier to keep because they don't need as much calcium and vitamin supplementation).

BRAZILIAN SLIDER

One of the most poorly understood sliders is *Trachemys dorbigni*. This is the southern-most member of the genus and also the most southern form of the *Chrysemys* mess. Its range is known to include southeastern Brazil and adjacent Argentina and Uruguay. Additionally, there are unproved reports of the species from southern Bolivia and Paraguay, as well as a perhaps introduced population in northeastern Brazil. The form is recognized as a species for convenience because its range is separated by a great distance (the entire Amazon basin) from the nearest Tropical Slider subspecies (*T. o. callirostris*). It bears a great resemblance to *callirostris* in the pattern of both the carapace and the plastron and has traces of the jaw ocelli of *callirostris* in the form of a single large yellow, black-edged spot extending back from the angle of the jaws; the chin is striped, not spotted. The carapace has curved yellow to orange lines on each vertebral (like reversed parentheses) and a dark spot on each costal surrounded by a complete or broken orange line, at

PHOTO: M. FREIBERG.

Dorsal view of a hatchling *T. d. brasiliensis*.

PHOTO: M. FREIBERG

Dorsal view of a hatchling *T. d. dorbigni*.

least in juveniles, while the plastron has a complicated pattern of dark lines and hollow ovals that becomes solid dark in adults.

The Brazilian Slider is smaller than many subspecies of Tropical Slider, only 10 inches (26 cm) in large females compared to as much as 15 or 16 inches (38 cm) in many Tropical Slider females. Curiously, the mature male (which often is melanistic) is reported to have elongated claws on the front feet like the Northern Slider and unlike the South American subspecies of the Tropical Slider. The habitat and feeding requirements of the species are like those of other sliders. In Argentina, females nest during December (at least) and may lay 15 or more eggs in a clutch; several clutches are laid in a season.

Brazilian Sliders once entered the pet market on a fairly regular basis, though they never were common. They fed on fish and invertebrates and did not seem to be any different in their keeping requirements from Northern Sliders.

CARIBBEAN SLIDERS

The islands of the Caribbean have their own group of sliders, which tend to be large (12 inches, 30 cm), blackish turtles that are poorly known biologically and only recently have become somewhat understood taxonomically. These species seldom have entered the pet hobby, but indications are that at least one species responds well to captivity. Because these turtles are unlikely to be seen in the hobby, are not especially attractive, and are poorly understood, I'll keep my coverage brief. Four species of Caribbean sliders now are recognized (plus an introduced population of *T. scripta elegans* in Guadeloupe).

PHOTO: DR. P. C. H. PRITCHARD.

Head view of *Trachemys terrapen* from Jamaica. Most adults of this species are very dark.

JAMAICAN SLIDER

Trachemys terrapen is found on Jamaica and also (probably introduced) in the northern Bahamas. It is a fairly large (females 11 inches, 27 cm; males 8 inches, 20 cm), dark species with a carapace that is flared at the back quarter and serrated on the back edge. The carapace is nearly black and often is covered with deep wrinkles, while the plastron is yellow and usually unmarked except for brown lines where the scutes meet. In specimens over two years old the yellow lines of the head are greatly reduced, being restricted mostly to four lines under the throat and indications of a couple more on the face and on the legs. Juveniles are greenish and have the plastron covered with a broad dull brown pattern that covers most of the undershell; there are round spots under the margins of the carapace.

The Jamaican Slider is found in many types of water on Jamaica, from ponds and lakes to streams. Males have long claws on their front feet that they wave over the face of the female before mating. Several clutches of three to eight eggs are laid each year in a shallow nest dug near the water.

Nesting occurs from about March through September. Hatchlings are relatively large (1.8 inches, 4 cm) and have a distinct keel on the carapace. These turtles feed on a variety of plants when adult, but seem to prefer custard apple (*Annona*), a widely distributed tropical fruit that grows from a large shrub commonly overhanging the water.

HISPANIOLAN SLIDER

Two sliders are found on the large island of Hispaniola, but only one is endemic. *Trachemys decorata* is restricted to southwestern Haiti, where it is fairly common in freshwater and brackish lakes. It is a large species, females reaching almost 14 inches (35 cm) in shell length and males a good deal smaller at just 9 inches (22 cm), with a pale brown carapace that is weakly serrated at the posterior edge. Often a distinct pattern can be recognized on the carapace, this consisting of a dark spot on each costal and marginal scute surrounded by an obvious yellowish circle. The plastron is yellow with many separate dark circles and ovals that rarely connect into a dark figure as in most sliders. The neck, face, and legs are marked with bright yellow stripes on a brownish to greenish ground color, the line behind the eye broadened and often bright yellow to pale green.

This can be a very pretty turtle, probably the nicest of the Caribbean sliders. Juveniles are especially brightly marked; they feed on insects, snails, and crustaceans. Adults of course have more muted patterns and gradually switch over to a more herbivorous diet. In captivity specimens have eaten a broad variety of plants and animals, much like the Red-eared Slider. Males have long front claws. Females lay clutches of six to 18 eggs between April and July, usually producing two or three clutches each year. The eggs incubate between two and three months.

Of all the Caribbean sliders, this seems to be the most adaptable to captivity as well as the prettiest. Captives are said to be quite tame and easy to handle. Unfortunately, it seldom is available.

PHOTO: DR. P. C. H. PRITCHARD.

Trachemys decorata, the Hispaniolan Slider, may be the most attractive Caribbean slider. It occasionally is available in the pet trade.

CUBAN SLIDER

Found over most of the island of Cuba and its satellite islands, including the Caymans, is *Trachemys decussata*, sometimes known as the North Antillean Slider or the West Indian Slider; the common name Cuban Slider seems much more appropriate, however. Adults are dark, not especially attractive turtles in which females reach almost 16 inches (39 cm) and males are also large, over 11 inches (28 cm) in shell length. Adults

PHOTO: DR. P. C. H. PRITCHARD.

A pretty hatchling of the Caymans subspecies of the Cuban Slider, *Trachemys decussata angusta*, formerly known as *T. granti*.

(especially males) may be almost uniformly dark and lack distinctive patterns. Juveniles are brightly marked with a dark spot on each costal and marginal scute encircled by a yellow to orangish line and have a broad yellow stripe behind the eye with a pink to orange center; the plastron is bright yellow with a symmetrical dark figure following the seams of the scutes. Typical adults have a dark brownish carapace, unmarked yellow plastron, and dark brown to black skin with weak yellow stripes on the face and throat and traces of yellow stripes on the legs. Typically the sides of the carapace are parallel or slightly pinched in at the center (in the very similar *T. stejnegeri* the carapace tends to be broadest at the center, not pinched in). Populations from western Cuba, the Isle of Pines, and the Caymans are considered a distinct subspecies, *T. d. angusta*, on the basis of small differences in shell and skull proportions.

Cuban Sliders live in almost all types of water available as long as it is not moving fast. They even live well in brackish lakes and the mouths of rivers. Males have long foreclaws that they vibrate in the female's face before mating. Nesting seems to peak during the rainy season, May to July, with hatching from July to September at the end of the rainy period. Females lay clutches of about five eggs. Turtle eggs are a favored food of the human population, so nesting success may be quite limited. Hatchlings are a bit over an inch (3 cm) long and grow slowly, reaching sexual maturity at 5 inches (13 cm) in males and 8 inches (19 cm) in females in about four to five years. As expected, juveniles are more carnivorous than the mostly herbivorous adults.

CENTRAL ANTILLEAN SLIDER

Trachemys stejnegeri is an odd Caribbean slider in which the snout is distinctly elongated in the male, much like most sliders from Central America. Adults are rather small for the area (males 8 inches, 20 cm; females 11 inches, 28 cm) and have brownish carapaces with little or no pattern; the plastron is yellow with at least traces of a symmetrical dark pattern of connected ovals along the seams.

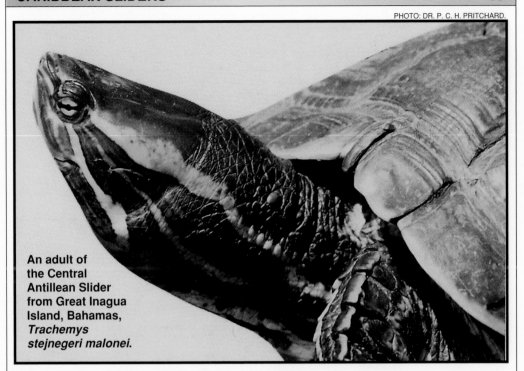

PHOTO: DR. P. C. H. PRITCHARD.

An adult of the Central Antillean Slider from Great Inagua Island, Bahamas, *Trachemys stejnegeri malonei.*

The stripe behind the eye is wide and dull reddish brown to bright red, much like an old Red-eared Slider. Juveniles and hatchlings are more colorful, sometimes with orange plastra and dark spots encircled by orange lines on the marginals. Three subspecies are recognized on technical grounds for the three major populations of the species. *T. s. stejnegeri* occurs on Puerto Rico, *T. s. vicina* lives in the eastern part of Hispaniola, and *T. s. malonei* is found only on Great Inagua Island in the southern Bahamas.

Males have elongated front claws, like the other Caribbean and the North American sliders, that they vibrate in front of a female's face before mating. Nesting runs from about April to at least July, with one to three clutches of about six eggs being deposited. The eggs hatch after two to three months. As usual, juveniles are more carnivorous than adults, but even adults of this species readily take snails, crustaceans, aquatic insects, and pieces of fish. Though widely distributed (and often of local economic importance for the eggs and edible flesh), there is little hobby experience with the Central Antillean Slider.

No one is sure how *T. stejnegeri malonei* got to the freshwater ponds on Great Inagua Island. It may have been introduced by Amerindians a few hundred years ago.

PHOTO: DR. P. C. H. PRITCHARD.

THE NEGLECTED CHICKENS

In all the flurry of attention given to the Red-eared Slider and the various cooters in the terrarium hobby, few hobbyists have ever kept or even seen a Chicken Turtle. Though I find Chickens to be very interesting animals in many respects, they have never gotten their due from either hobbyists or scientists. Though they are relatively common in much of the southeastern United States westward into the Mississippi Valley and eastern Texas, little has been published about them.

The Chicken Turtle, *Deirochelys reticularia*, is the poor cousin of the mysterious sliders and cooters. Though described by Latreille in 1802, for many years it was considered a rare species. Even when I was growing up in Louisiana in the 1950's it was considered an event to find a Chicken, though later it was realized that they were just more secretive than the common sliders and cooters. Chicken

Turtles just seem to like to keep a low profile in shallow, usually non-moving but not dirty water, often where the vegetation near the shore is quite dense and the bottom soft. I've often found them in roadside ditches with just a few inches of water, and I've seen them basking in borrow pits (holes dug to remove dirt used for road construction) along with sliders and cooters; I even vividly remember running over a few while mowing the front yard near a roadside ditch when I was a kid (an experience that I do not recommend to anyone).

PHOTO: R. D. BARTLETT.

The Chicken Turtle from Florida, *Deirochelys reticularia chrysea*, is distinctively marked and almost the only form to be seen in the herp hobby.

RECOGNITION

Chickens look like Painted Turtles with extremely long necks. Both the skull and the neck itself are elongated, often equalling the length of the plastron and being three-quarters the length of the carapace. The back of the skull is especially long, and the whole head appears narrow, with a long, pointed snout. This is the only American emydid turtle that has the first vertebral scute widened enough to come into contact with four marginal scutes. The carapace is low, brownish to greenish in color, lacks a keel in adults, is covered with fine wrinkles, and has a smooth back edge without serrations (much like a Paint), while the plastron is bright yellow with few or no black markings. The pattern on the legs is distinctive: the front legs each have one wide bright yellow stripe, while the backs of the thighs are bright yellow with narrow black *vertical* stripes (the "striped pants"). The bright stripes with their distinctive placements probably help the Chickens tell themselves from the cooters and sliders with which they often are found.

In specimens from Florida and from west of the Mississippi River the shell has a distinctive open network of intermeshing orange or

PHOTO: R. D. BARTLETT.

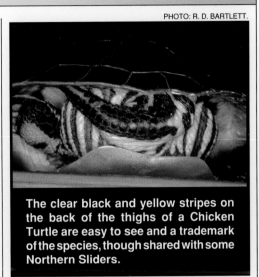

The clear black and yellow stripes on the back of the thighs of a Chicken Turtle are easy to see and a trademark of the species, though shared with some Northern Sliders.

yellow lines and a bright yellow or orange rim. Specimens from the southeastern United States (except Florida) are much duller, the yellow lines of the carapace often being almost invisible in adults unless they are washed or submerged and the rim being at best dull yellowish. Specimens from east of the Mississippi River have the head blackish with bright green to yellow-green stripes (more stripes in the Florida form) and have similar stripes on the throat and chin. In western specimens the chin and throat lack yellowish stripes or just have vague traces of stripes; the western form also has a lot of black on the plastron that is absent from the eastern forms.

These differences in color pattern have led to the description of three subspecies of Chicken Turtles. Those from peninsular Florida are *Deirochelys reticularia chrysea*, the other specimens from east of the Mississippi River being *D. r. reticularia*. Specimens from west of the Mississippi River

Chickens are pretty turtles when in good condition, and the Florida *D. r. chrysea* is especially nice. Notice the broad bright yellow band across the front leg, a character found only in the Chicken Turtle.

PHOTO: R. D. BARTLETT.

(and, oddly, northwestern Mississippi) are known as *D. r. miaria*. The natural history of all the subspecies seems to be similar as far as known (which, admittedly, is not very far).

NATURAL HISTORY

Chickens are turtles of still or slow waters, and they spend much of their day basking along with other aquatic turtles, but they are much shyer than typical cooters and sliders, slipping into the water before they can be observed for very long. Often they venture well away from the water, however, and it is not uncommon to find a specimen moving across a field or a highway on the way from one ditch or pond to another. As you might imagine, highway deaths are fairly common. Basking turtles seem to attain a core temperature of about 77°F (25°C), and they are not especially hot baskers.

Juveniles (which are very brightly marked in all the subspecies) are cute little 1-inch (2.5-cm) turtles, swinging their long heads and necks around while searching for small prey. The young feed almost exclusively on snails, small shrimp and crayfish, scuds, isopods, other crustacean, and aquatic insects of various types. They also will take earthworms and their aquatic relatives. The young grow fairly fast (about an inch a year) for the first several years until they approach about 4 inches (10 cm) carapace length in males and 6 inches (15 cm) in females. Hatchlings have a low keel down the center of the carapace, but this rapidly disappears with growth. The maximum shell size is 10 inches (25 cm), but this is rare; females, as usual in this group of turtles, are larger than males.

Adults have a bit broader dietary limits than young, taking mostly animal foods (including frogs, fish, and the decaying chicken used to bait fish traps) as well as some vegetation. The long neck and head allow them to poke their snouts into hidden spots at the base of plants and under debris in search of prey during the early hours of the morning and late afternoons.

Except in peninsular Florida, where they are active all year, Chicken Turtles hibernate during the winter, hiding under mud and debris at the bottom of ponds and ditches. They usually come out by March or so and remain active until October or later, depending on the locality.

BREEDING

Females are mature at a shell size of about 6 inches (15 cm) and probably three years of age, while males are ready to breed at only 3 inches (7.5 cm) when only two years old. They typically live for over 15 years and may reach almost 25 years of age, probably laying at least one clutch each year after they reach maturity.

As in other non-tropical sliders and cooters, a male Chicken Turtle courts females by moving the long claws of his front feet in front of the female's face before moving behind her to mount and mate. Males have longer tails than females and a concave posterior plastron.

Typically Chicken Turtles lay

during two periods, once in spring (March to May, sometimes earlier) and once in late autumn (August to November), except in Florida, where the turtles may nest from September to March. They are adapted to lay in cool weather, and at least in some situations the eggs stop developing shortly after being laid (a diapause) until they are subjected to chilling, which returns the embryo to active cell division. This should be remembered if you ever try to breed Chickens that don't come from Florida. Usually there are eight eggs in a clutch, each about 0.75 to 1 inch (1.8 to 2.5 cm) wide and as much as 1.5 inches (4 cm) long. Some females appear to hold the shelled eggs for long periods (up to eight months) inside the shell before laying them, while others lay within two weeks of the shell being produced over the egg. Eggs are laid in a typical goblet-shaped nest dug in loose soil near water.

Incubation times vary considerably with temperature and geography, from about five months in the Carolinas to under three months in Florida. In at least some instances the hatchlings remain in the nest over the winter if the weather has become too cold by the time they hatch. Usually the hatching of both spring-laid and autumn-laid clutches is correlated with an abundance of food for the hatchlings.

KEEPING

Though some Chicken Turtles are nasty, vicious animals that use their long necks to reach almost to the back of the shell and bite the hands that hold them (be warned!), others are rather gentle and more interested in escape than biting. Like other aquatic turtles, they are dirty feeders and require a large aquarium with strong filtration. The water must be kept exceptionally clean or they will come down with a bacterial shell rot that rapidly disfigures the shell and may eventually lead to death.

This is a thin-shelled turtle, but it still needs a stable basking area under a spotlight for at least ten hours a day, accompanied by full-

Even though Chicken Turtles are not especially hot baskers, they still need good lighting from a full-spectrum basking lamp several hours a day. Photo courtesy of Coralife/Energy Savers.

PHOTO: R. D. BARTLETT.

A hatchling *Deirochelys reticularia chrysea*. In this subspecies the adult retains most of the bright colors of the young, at least some of the time.

spectrum fluorescent light. The food (crustaceans are to be preferred to fish if you can get them) should be liberally laced with calcium and vitamin supplements if you are trying to raise a young specimen. Remember that in nature the young grow about an inch a year, and aim for that rate in the aquarium.

Because the animals often stay shy and want to wander away from the aquarium, they should be approached slowly and the tank should always be covered. A panicked fall from 4 feet will certainly not help the turtle. Remember that the eggs may need to be chilled for a night or two to allow them to develop fully.

Although I personally like Chicken Turtles, I like to see them in the wild. They probably are not suitable pets for beginners or moderately advanced hobbyists, if

for no other reason than it is almost impossible to keep the aquarium clean enough to avoid shell rot. You might, however, be able to adapt them from a fish and crustacean diet to a diet based on mice and trout chow, which *might* reduce the amount of dirt to be filtered from the water.

Florida Chickens are rather high-domed compared to specimens from the western part of the range and have a narrow orange line around the edge of the carapace.

PHOTO: DR. P. C. H. PRITCHARD